GETTING TO KNOW
THE WORLD'S
GREATEST COMPOSERS

P E T E R
TCHAIKOVSKY

WRITTEN AND ILLUSTRATED BY MIKE VENEZIA

CONSULTANTS

DONALD FREUND, PROFESSOR OF COMPOSITION, INDIANA UNIVERSITY SCHOOL OF MUSIC
AMELIA S. KAPLAN, M.A. IN COMPOSITION AND MUSICOLOGY, THE UNIVERSITY OF CHICAGO

CHILDRENS PRESS®
CHICAGO

*To my grade school, high-school, and college
teachers—the good ones who made a difference.*

Picture Acknowledgments
Music on cover and title page, Stock Montage, Inc.; 3, North
Wind Picture Archives; 6, courtesy The National Ballet of
Canada/photograph © B. Gray; 7 (top), © Costas; 7 (bottom),
courtesy The National Ballet of Canada/photograph © B. Gray;
12-13, Stock Montage, Inc.; 20-21, Russian State Museum, St.
Petersburg, Russia/Scala/Art Resource, NY; 23, Stock Montage,
Inc.; 30, North Wind Picture Archives; 31, courtesy The National
Ballet of Canada/photograph © C. Von Tiedemann; 32, © Costas

Project Editor: Shari Joffe
Design: PCI Design Group, San Antonio, Texas
Photo Research: Jan Izzo

Library of Congress Cataloging–in–Publication Data

Venezia, Mike.
    Peter Tchaikovsky / written and illustrated by Mike Venezia.
    p.   cm. -- (Getting to know the world's greatest composers)
    ISBN 0-516-04537-7
    1. Tchaikovsky, Peter Ilich, 1840-1893--Juvenile literature.
    2. Composers--Russia--Biography--Juvenile literature.
    [1. Tchaikovsky, Peter Ilich, 1840-1893. 2. Composers.] I. Title.
    II. Series.
    ML3930.C4V46   1994
    780' .92--dc20
    [B]   94-9479
                                     CIP
                                     AC MN

Peter Ilich Tchaikovsky

Peter Tchaikovsky was born in the Russian town of Votkinsk in 1840. He used his great imagination to create beautiful music that was sometimes very happy and sometimes very sad.

Peter wrote his music during a time known as the Romantic period. The music written by Romantic composers wasn't necessarily about falling in

love—but about their own dream world and deepest feelings. When you listen to Peter Tchaikovsky's music, you can often tell how he felt while he was writing it.

Romantic
composers
sometimes wrote
their music to go
along with a
well-known
story or poem.
Tchaikovsky's
three ballets,
Swan Lake,
Sleeping Beauty,
and *The*
Nutcracker, all
came from
popular stories.

A scene from *The Nutcracker*,
as performed by the
National Ballet of Canada

A scene from *Swan Lake*,
as performed by the
New York City Ballet

A scene from *Sleeping Beauty*,
as performed by the
National Ballet of Canada

Peter Tchaikovsky first became interested in music when he was four or five years old. One day, Peter's father brought home an orchestrion, a machine that played music. It was like a giant music box with lots of additional parts, so it sounded more like a real orchestra.

One of the pieces the orchestrion played was a tune by Wolfgang Amadeus Mozart. He was a famous Austrian composer who had lived during the 1700s, before Peter was born.

Peter loved Mozart's music. He tried
to copy the pieces he heard from the
orchestrion on his family's piano.

While Peter was growing up, he was very sensitive. Things that wouldn't bother most children seemed like the worst thing in the world to Peter.

Being supersensitive was always a problem for Peter Tchaikovsky, but it was also one of the reasons he was able to write such beautiful music.

Peter had feelings about things that
most people didn't even think about. He
was able to put those feelings into his music.

As a young man, Peter Tchaikovsky didn't start out to become a serious composer. Even though he wrote some pieces and played the piano and flute pretty well, music was really more of a hobby than a career. At the time when Peter was growing up, hardly anyone in Russia made a living by writing music.

In fact, Peter's parents had always planned for him to become a lawyer. When he was ten years old, his parents decided he should begin learning about law. They sent him to a few different schools in St. Petersburg, the city where they lived. When Peter was twenty-one,

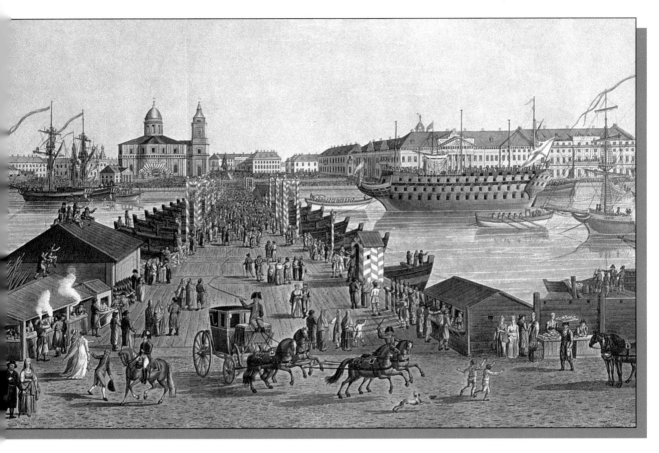

St. Petersburg in 1803

he graduated from law school, and took
a job in a government office.

During Peter's time, when it came to
serious classical music, people in Russia
were satisfied listening to the music of
composers from Italy, France, Austria,
Germany, and other parts of Europe.

Fortunately for Peter, things were starting to change in Russia. There was a group of people in St. Petersburg who thought it was about time that Russia had its own music, written by Russia's own composers.

Soon after Peter started his job, a new music school opened up in St. Petersburg. Since music was practically all Peter could think about, and since he didn't

really like his job that much, he
thought it might be a good time to quit
and start studying music seriously at
the new school.

One of Peter's teachers at the school was a famous musician named Anton Rubinstein. Anton knew Peter could become a great composer someday, and worked hard with him to develop his talents. Later, when Anton's equally famous brother, Nikolai, started a new music school in the city of Moscow, Peter was invited to join him as a teacher. Peter was able to make a small salary

while continuing to learn about music from Nikolai.

Both Anton and Nikolai were very tough on Peter. They often criticized his music as a way of making sure Peter was doing the best work he could. Although Peter didn't like to be criticized, he learned a lot from the two brothers, and ended up becoming friends with them.

It wasn't long before Peter Tchaikovsky started to do very well with his music. Once, he was asked to conduct one of his pieces for an audience. Peter was so nervous, he imagined his head might fall off, and held tightly to his beard through the entire performance.

It took ten years before Peter felt he could conduct in front of an audience again.

Peter was always getting upset about
things that were completely imaginary.

Carnival of 1916, a wintry Russian landscape by Boris Kustodiev

Peter worked so hard on his music that he sometimes made himself sick. When he was writing his first symphony, he worked night and day until he wore himself out trying to get it just the way he wanted. Peter named his first symphony *Winter Dreams.* When you listen to it, you can almost see wintry fields, and imagine the feeling of riding a horse-drawn sleigh over the snowy Russian countryside

that Peter loved so much. *Winter Dreams* (also called Symphony No. 1 in G Minor) is a good example of how Peter Tchaikovsky was able to put what he felt or dreamt about into music.

Peter also included melodies from Russian folk songs in his first symphony. He had always enjoyed listening to folk songs when he was little.

Peter listened carefully when he heard working people whistling outside his window or children singing while playing in the streets. He wrote down some of these folk tunes, and used them in his later symphonies, operas, and ballets.

Many Romantic composers got musical ideas from their country's folk songs and peasant dances. Composers like Franz Liszt,

An 1800 engraving of Russian
peasants doing traditional folk dances

Frédéric Chopin, Edvard Grieg, and
Nikolai Rimsky-Korsakov all used folk
music to add excitement to their music
and show how proud they were of their
countries and their histories.

By the time Peter was thirty-seven years old, he had written three operas, three symphonies, one ballet, and lots of other musical pieces. Sometimes his music was well liked, but many times, people didn't care for it at all. Peter was upset by this as well as by the fact that he wasn't making very much money.

Just when Peter was starting to worry about his future, an amazing thing happened! A rich widow who loved Peter's music decided to help him out. Madam Nadezhda von Meck wanted Peter to be able to work on his music without worrying about money or having to get another job. She agreed to give Peter money every year, as long as they would never meet each other face

to face. Peter went along with Madam
von Meck's wishes, and as strange as it
seems, they became best friends by
writing each other letters for many
years. In fact, Peter dedicated his
famous Symphony No. 4 in F Minor to
Madam von Meck.

Peter Tchaikovsky had always loved to travel. Now that he had more money, he felt better about taking trips all over Europe. He sometimes gave concerts in the cities he visited. His travels also gave him ideas for new music.

Peter was very close to his family, especially his brother, Modeste, and his sister, Sasha. Peter often traveled with Modeste.

On one trip to Paris, France, Peter heard a newly invented instrument called a celesta. It looked like a small piano, but made a beautiful bell-like sound.

Peter thought it would be a perfect
instrument to add to his new *Nutcracker
Suite*. Peter wanted to be the first
composer to use the celesta, and had one
secretly smuggled out of Paris. You can
hear its magical bell-like sound throughout
the "Dance of the Sugar Plum Fairy."

One of Peter Tchaikovsky's talents was discovering new instruments, and using unusual new combinations of instruments to get beautiful and exciting sounds into his music.

In one of his most famous pieces, the *1812 Overture*, Peter even used church bells and real cannons to get just the right sound.

29

Peter Tchaikovsky

Even though Peter Tchaikovsky became famous all over the world for his music, he was very unhappy much of the time. One of his biggest problems was that he could never find the right person to fall in love with. Peter felt like he was missing out on one of the most important parts of his life. Peter beautifully expressed his troubled feelings in the very last piece he composed, Symphony No. 6 in B Minor (also known as the *Pathétique*).

He did seem to find happiness, though, composing music about love. Some of the most beautiful love music ever written can be heard in Tchaikovsky's *Romeo and Juliet* overture and in his ballet *Sleeping Beauty*.

A scene from *Sleeping Beauty*, as performed by the National Ballet of Canada

A scene from *The Nutcracker*, as performed by the New York City Ballet

Peter Tchaikovsky lived to be fifty-three years old. Probably one of the most important things he gave to his music was beautiful and interesting melodies. A melody is the tune—the part of a musical piece that's easiest to remember. It's usually the part that's most fun to hum or whistle. Two of Peter Tchaikovsky's best loved pieces, Violin Concerto in D Major and Piano Concerto No. 1 in B-flat Minor, are filled with beautiful melodies.

It's pretty easy to find Peter Tchaikovsky's music on public radio and television stations. During the holiday season, many ballet companies across the country put on performances of *The Nutcracker*.